Rock Star –
New Discovery

Ginni Light and
Annie Broadhead

Rock Star –
New Discovery

ELT

For Jade

PENGUIN BOOKS

Published by the Penguin Group
27 Wrights Lane, London W8 5TZ, England
Viking Penguin Inc., 40 West 23rd Street, New York, New York 10010, USA
Penguin Books Australia Ltd, Ringwood, Victoria, Australia
Penguin Books Canada Ltd, 2801 John Street, Markham, Ontario, Canada L3R 1B4
Penguin Books (NZ) Ltd, 182–190 Wairau Road, Auckland 10, New Zealand

Penguin Books Ltd, Registered Offices: Harmondsworth, Middlesex, England

First published by Penguin Books 1989
13579108642

Copyright © Ginni Light and Annie Broadhead, 1989
All rights reserved
Illustrations by Richardson Freelance

Typeset in 11/14 pt Linotron 202 Zapf Book Light

Made and printed in Great Britain by
Hazell Watson & Viney Limited
Member of BPCC plc
Aylesbury, Bucks, England

CONTENTS

INTRODUCTION

Adventure Gamebooks allow readers to take part in their own story. At the end of many of the sections readers are asked to make a choice. They then turn to the relevant section to continue their own particular story.

Each book consists of a series of interwoven short stories. Readers will not usually read the whole of each book, but, by making their own choices, read one of the short stories.

Readers can then go back and make different choices and give their story a different direction. In this way the book can be extended, or reused, and the stories become quite different.

1

You love rock music; you spend all your spare time singing. You think you have a very good voice and that you are good enough to sing in a rock group. Your parents do not agree and think that you should work harder at school. You hate school – you think it is very boring and you prefer singing to doing your homework. All your friends think that you are mad and that you will never join a rock group. Your favourite group is the Tektroniks and their pictures are all over your bedroom wall.

One day, on your way to school, you see a poster advertising a talent contest for singers. The judges are the Tektroniks. The contest is in the next town on 6 May. You get an entry form. You do not know if you are going to fill it in and post it.

If you decide to post it, turn to **38**. If you decide not to post it, turn to **11**.

You have got a letter from Phonograph! You are jumping up and down with excitement as you open the letter. Your mother is standing there and she is watching you. You open the letter and read it out loud to her:

Dear Fonzi,

We would like you to come into our recording studios and test your voice. We will make a demo record and see how it goes. Please be at our studios on 2nd July at 9 a.m.

You cannot read the signature but it does not matter. You turn to your mother and you say, 'Gosh! How exciting! Mum, I've done it! I've done it!'

Your mother feels very excited too, then she says, 'But Fonzi, you can't go on that day. It's your Mathematics exam in the morning and your English exam in the afternoon.'

You say, 'But I have to go. It's a brilliant opportunity. Never mind the exams, I must go!'

She says, 'I think you should wait and talk to your father.'

You feel really cross – how could she think of exams when you have an opportunity to go to the recording studios! If you decide to go straight to your room and sulk, turn to **10**. If you decide to wait and see your father, turn to **46**.

You decided to answer. You think things are difficult enough. Someone bangs on the door again. You open it. It is your teacher. 'Fonzi, are you all right? What are you doing in there? Come on, it's time for your English lesson.'

You arrive five minutes late in the classroom. There is loud music playing. It's the Beatles. You are very surprised.

'Ah, there you are Fonzi. Go and sit down quickly. Today, we are having a lesson on the Beatles,' says your English teacher. Your lesson is all about the song 'When I'm sixty-four'. You really enjoy it, you think it's great. At the end of the lesson you all sing the song.

Your teacher says, 'Who's singing in that fantastic voice? Is that you, Fonzi?'

You turn the colour of a tomato – you blush and say, 'Yes, it's me.'

Your teacher asks you, 'Have you ever sung with a band? I think you should!'

All the other kids are now leaving the classroom because it is the end of the lesson. If you decide to tell your teacher all about the talent contest, turn to **65**. If you decide not to tell your teacher, turn to **48**.

4

You decided to go and see your headmaster. He says, 'Come in, Fonzi. Sit down and tell me why you have not been working lately! Your school marks are terrible. I really am very disappointed.'

Suddenly, all your self-confidence disappears. You mutter, 'Er ... er ... well ... you see, I really don't think school work is very important. You see, I *did* win the talent contest and I *am* going to make a record, so I don't really see much point in studying – and I don't really like it!'

You have said absolutely the wrong thing. Your headmaster goes red in the face and starts shouting at you. You know that what he is saying is right and sensible. You should work and concentrate on both your studies and your music. You really made a wrong decision. Go back to **25** and try again!

5

You decided to post the letter to the studios asking for a different date. You do not really want to but you must take your examinations. You go to school and you try to work hard. You would like to continue your education and at the same time you would like to make a record.

After a few days, another letter arrives from Phonograph suggesting a different date. Your father was right. You are very happy that you still have the chance to make a demo disc! The studio is even going to send a car to collect you. Great! Turn to **32**.

| 6 |

What an embarrassing situation you are in! What can you do? You are a long way from home, you are starving and would like something to eat but you have no money.

Well, you cannot lock yourself in the toilet this time! You search in your pockets for some money. You find some coins and you decide it would be a good idea to phone your father. You know he will help you but you also know that he will be very angry. You wish that your friends were with you. Paul, the singer from Tektroniks comes up to you, as you are standing by the telephone box and says, 'Hey, Fonzi! What's the matter? You look really worried! You've got nothing to worry about with a voice like yours. Come and sit down and we'll have a chat about your great future.'

You do not really want to explain your problem – you feel so silly! An hour passes. You have eaten something, as little as possible because you have no money and cannot pay for much food. You decide to try to phone your father again. Suddenly, the door to the restaurant opens – it is your father! Turn to **20**.

7

You decided not to answer. You stay in the cloak-room until you think everybody has gone away. You come out and look in the mirror. Your eyes are a bit red because you have been crying. You wonder what to do. 'Shall I go home? Shall I go to lessons?' you think.

You decide to go to the lesson. It is an English lesson and they are learning all about the Beatles! You are very surprised, especially when your teacher starts playing a cassette of 'When I'm sixty-four'. You listen and all of you learn the words. Then your teacher asks you all to sing the song. If you decide to join in, turn to **53**. If you decide not to join in, turn to **58**.

8

You decide to ring your parents and tell them what happened so that they do not worry. You think that you are probably in enough trouble at school already and you do not want to lie to your parents and create problems for yourself. Anyway, you hope that somebody will ring you next week about your win at the talent contest and you would like to have your family's support.

You get through to your home. Your father answers. He says, 'Where on earth are you, Fonzi? Your headmaster has already rung us and told us that you didn't come home with the school. You know, it's far too dangerous for you to be out on your own at this time.'

You say, 'Look, I'll explain everything later – but I've missed the train and I have to wait for two hours – '

Your father interrupts and says, 'Just stay there! Go and stay in the waiting room. I'm coming to collect you. A young girl can't be out alone these days.'

You are very fed up and feel like a little child but what are you going to do? You know the restaurant the Tektroniks have gone to. If you decide to go to the restaurant after all, turn to **90**. If you decide to wait for your father, turn to **86**.

9

Well, you made a big mistake. You should have gone home with the school. You should have listened to your friends and your headmaster. Now you feel terrible!

Your father says 'We're really very angry and upset with you, Fonzi. Why did you do this? You are much too young to be out at night like this and with a group of people like the Tektroniks! They're all much older than you. How can we trust you again? Your school work is not very good and it is very important to have a good career and a good education. We think your music must wait for a couple of years, until you finish school, and then we'll see!'

Oh dear! Your career seems to be over before it has begun. This is the end of the road for you. You should not have gone to the restaurant or the party – you should have gone back to your village. Perhaps you would like to go back and make some different decisions! ■

10

You decided to go to your room and sulk. You did not wait to see your father and discuss things with your parents. You feel really angry and really fed up.

Some time later, your father arrives. You can hear him talking to your mother. You try to listen to what they are saying, but you cannot.

You decide to go to bed and pretend to be asleep! You know your father will come to see you later. He comes to your room and switches on the light. He says, 'Now Fonzi, I know you're not asleep. You're sulking. Well, I think enough is enough. You have your exams on the same day as the appointment at the recording studio. Your exams are more important. You should concentrate on them. It's your future, you know.'

You say, 'But I really want to be a singer. I'm fed up with school, I'm fed up with homework and I'm fed up with exams!'

Your father says 'OK. That's enough for now, let's talk about it tomorrow.' Turn to **84**.

11

You decided not to post it. You sit at home looking at the pictures of the Tektroniks. You really want to meet them. You have every record they have made. Your friend Peter comes round to visit you. You say, 'Have you heard about the talent contest? Well, I've got the entry form. I've filled it in. What shall I do now?' Peter says 'You should post it. You've got a great voice. This could be your lucky chance.'

If you decide Peter is right and post the entry form, turn to **23**. If you decide Peter is wrong and do nothing, turn to **15**.

12

You decided to go and discuss it with your headmaster. You try and explain how much you would all like to go and how important it is.

He says, 'Fonzi, I feel we have all really encouraged you. You know that it is very unusual for the school to come to a talent contest! I feel we've done everything to help you – now I think we should come down to earth! Come on, let's get on our way home and we'll celebrate on the way!'

You feel a bit fed up about this and think your headmaster is wrong, but you do as he says and soon you are on your way home. You laugh and joke with your friends and you all have a good singsong together. Everyone joins in – even your headmaster!

You go home and life continues as usual, you go to school, do your work, go and visit your friends. You made the right decision.

One day when you get home from school your mother is holding a letter and smiling. She is obviously waiting for you. You have got a letter from Phonograph, the recording company! Great! Turn to **2**.

13

You walk into the school building. You try to ignore your friends but they are still shouting at you. You turn round and stick out your tongue at them. They run into the school after you and they chase you down the corridor. You are all running and making a terrible noise. You are supposed to be very quiet inside the school.

Unfortunately, you run straight into the headmaster. He says, 'Why were you running? You know you shouldn't run inside the school.' You say 'Er . . . er.' You cannot think of an excuse. He says, 'Come on, Fonzi. Tell me why you were running.'

You explain everything to him and you finish by saying, '. . . and I am number thirty-seven. I am so excited.' Fortunately for you, your headmaster loves music and he says, 'Of course you can have the afternoon off school. You can go to the talent contest. Not only that, we will all come and see you.'

You thank him, you now feel very embarrassed because everybody is coming to see you. Turn to **42**.

You gave a sensible answer. The following day, you and your father go to the school to see your headmaster. Your father explains the situation – your appointment at the studios is at the same time as your English and Maths exams. He asks the headmaster for advice.

Your headmaster asks you, 'What do you think would be best for you, Fonzi?'

You say, 'Well, of course, I'd love to go to the studios but I know I need to take the exams too. Both are really important!'

Your father looks very pleased as he listens to your answer. He says, 'Your behaviour has been a bit difficult lately, but that is a very sensible decision'.

Your headmaster thinks for a minute and then he says, 'I am prepared to make an exception and let you take the exams one day early. But you must promise not to phone your friends and tell them what the questions are.'

He shakes your father's hand and wishes you good luck. You thank him – you actually feel like giving him a big kiss but of course you cannot. Turn to **88**.

15

You feel very down, everybody is talking about the talent contest tomorrow and you want to take part in it. All your friends have decided to go and see it.

When you get home from school, there is a letter for you. Your mother asks, 'What is that?'

You open it. It says that you are number thirty-seven in the talent contest. You realize Peter secretly posted your entry form. You feel very excited. You say to your mother, 'I am in the talent contest. I'm number thirty-seven. Are you going to come and see me?'

Your mother says, 'You must be mad! You aren't good enough. Anyway, you're still at school. You're too young.'

You feel very angry with her. If you decide not to go, turn to **33**. If you decide to go, turn to **42**.

16

You decided you did not want to talk to Peter. You are really loving the special treatment you are getting at school. You decide your friends do not understand you. You do not spend very much time with them any more and spend more time with another group of kids at school. Unfortunately for you, this other group of kids never does any work at school and think that it is great to do absolutely no studying and no homework. You start to behave in the same way.

One day, your headmaster sends a message that he wants to speak to you. Your new friend, the leader of this group of kids says to you, 'Hey, Fonzi, just don't go and see the headmaster. What can he do? Nothing, huh!'

You do not know what to do. You know that if you do not go and see him then you will have a problem. But you really do not want to see him because you have done no work at school. If you decide to go and see him, turn to **4**. If you decide not to go and see him, turn to **24**.

17

Your father is going to help you. He goes to the school in the morning with you and goes to talk to both your headmaster and your class teacher.

You wait anxiously. You can't concentrate on your lessons. You are waiting for break-time. You wonder what will happen. Peter says to you, 'Don't worry, I am sure it's all going to be alright!'

Break-time comes – your father and headmaster are waiting for you outside the classroom. They are both smiling. Your headmaster says, 'Well, we have decided you can go if you promise to work harder

at school, especially at Mathematics.'

You are delighted. You are over the moon. You do not even think about your Mathematics – you jump up and down with happiness. You run off to find your friend Peter, 'I'm going. I'm going!' you shout as soon as you find him. Your friends all crowd round you, 'Oh! That's great. I wish we could come. Then we could cheer you on!'

You think that is a wonderful idea – you would love to have them there. If you decide to go and ask your headmaster if they can come, turn to **26**. If you decide not to ask your headmaster, turn to **19**.

18

You decide to stay in the cloakroom and miss your turn on stage. You feel quite sick with nerves and you wonder what your friends will say.

Suddenly, Peter, your best friend comes running in and says, 'Come on. What's the matter with you? It's your turn next. Hurry up!'

You say 'I can't. I really can't. I'm not good enough. I'll just make an idiot of myself.'

Peter says, 'Come on. Don't be so stupid. You are

really good! Come on, go out there and show them! Nobody is going to come into the cloakroom to listen to you, you know!'

You laugh, Peter always makes you feel better. You decide to go and show everyone what you can do. Turn to **21**.

19

You decided not to ask your headmaster. Instead, you go home and worry about going on your own. Your mother asks you, 'What are you worrying about? You're going and that's what you wanted. Anyway I don't think it is as important as school!'

You disagree and you say politely, 'But Mum, it is a really good chance. I can't go without my friends. I'll feel really nervous, I won't be able to sing!'

She says, 'Nonsense. It doesn't make any difference whether your friends are there or not. At least they aren't thinking about silly music all the time. They're working hard at school.'

You know that is not true, but you cannot be bothered to argue. When your father comes home, you thank him for speaking to the headmaster and explain the problem about your friends. He says, 'If it's so important, go and talk to the headmaster.'

You decide you cannot do that and you just go on worrying. Turn to **30**.

20

Your father walks in. He comes over to you and says, 'On your feet, Fonzi! You're going home!' He is obviously very, very angry. You stand up, ready to go. What else can you do?

Everybody says, 'Bye bye Fonzi', 'Well done!', 'See you soon', 'Good luck with the record', and so on. They don't seem to understand the problem.

Your father ignores everybody and walks out of the restaurant. He gets into the car, and leans over and opens the door for you. You get in – he says, 'Fonzi, your mother and I are so disappointed with you. Your headmaster telephoned us. How could you do this? We've all supported you. Well, this is absolutely enough – it's the end! . . .' He continues like this for most of the journey home!

You feel so ashamed. You realize you have made a really big mistake. Perhaps you are not ready to make a record yet – perhaps it is too early for you. Probably it is better for you to wait until you are a bit older and able to make the right decisions.

Well, this is the end of the road for you – maybe you would like to go back and try some other decisions and see what happens! ■

21

It is your turn. You have been looking at your heroes, the Tektroniks, on stage. They look very far away and small, like little dots.

'Number thirty-seven. On stage, please!'

It is you. You get up. Your friends give you a thumbs up sign, your headmaster and English teacher smile encouragingly at you. 'Good luck, good luck,' everyone says.

You walk slowly towards the stage and climb the steps. You hope you will not trip and fall flat on your face in front of everyone. You have already arranged that you are going to sing your favourite rock song – a song which has both a fast part and a slower one which will show off your voice. A guitarist is going to accompany you.

You are on stage – the Tektroniks smile at you (yes, they are actually smiling at you!) The guitarist comes forward. Someone gives you a microphone. The music starts, you begin and somehow as you get into the music, your nerves disappear. You sing as you have never sung before – you really enjoy it.

Suddenly, to your surprise, you've finished and the audience is clapping. You hear people shouting, 'Yeah, great! Hooray!'

One of the Tektroniks walks up to you and says, 'Thank you. That was good!' You walk down the steps and go back to your seat in a dream. Your friends

congratulate you, 'Well done Fonzi. You were really marvellous.'

You settle down and listen to the rest of the concert. Turn to **47**.

22

Your father gets up and says to the Tektroniks, 'Thank you very much for looking after my daughter.'

You feel very young and rather silly, and you are also very tired. It has been a long, long day. You say, 'Goodbye' and leave.

You get into the car with your father. He is very quiet and you can tell that he is rather angry. You feel a bit afraid when you remember what you have done. Turn to **9**.

23

You always get up early to go to school. Every morning, you look at your posters of the Tektroniks and you think, 'I'm really going to see them soon. I can't wait.' You watch for the postman every day. You keep hoping there will be a letter for you. Every morning you look and every morning there is no letter for you.

But ... today the postman gives you a big smile and hands you a letter. He knows you have been waiting for something. You feel very excited. You tear open the letter – here it is – the information about the talent contest. You are number thirty-seven.

You hurry to get to school – you are a bit late but you do not care. You tell your friends, 'I'm in it! I'm number thirty-seven.'

Your friends ask you, 'In what? What?' They do not know what you are talking about. You explain. They say, 'Wow! We want to come and see you. We enjoy a good laugh!'

You get very angry and start shouting at them, 'You are just jealous. You can't sing. Leave me alone, you idiots!'

Your friends shout back at you. If you don't take any notice of them, turn to **13**. If you get really angry and start shouting back even louder, turn to **51**.

24

You decided not to go and see your headmaster. You decided to listen to your new group of friends.

When you go home that afternoon, your mother and father are waiting for you. Your mother looks very upset and your father looks extremely angry.

He says, 'I've just had a phone call from the school. What on earth do you think you are doing? You know, or you should know, that a good education is very important. Your music will never be as valuable as a good education. I'm waiting for an explanation from you about your behaviour and it had better be a good one.'

You feel quite shocked and your immediate re-action is to cry. What do you do – do you answer your father and try to explain? Turn to **41**. Or do you run up to your room in tears? Turn to **74**.

25

So you decided to be sensible and came home with your father. You feel very happy and relaxed. After all, you won the talent contest and you had no prob-lems with your parents or with your school – great!

You go back to school. All your friends think that you are wonderful and your classmates look at you with respect. You notice younger kids pointing at you in the school and lots of them come up and talk to you, or try to talk to you. Even your headmaster and your teachers talk to you and congratulate you. You are getting really special treatment and you love it. You feel like a star!

Your friend Peter comes to you one lunchtime a couple of days later and says, 'Fonzi, I think that you are getting too big-headed. Nothing has happened yet. Can I have a chat with you?' If you decide to talk

to him, even though you do not particularly want to, turn to **56**. If you decide you do not want to talk to him, turn to **16**.

26

You decided to ask your headmaster. You go and see him and say, 'Please, can all my friends come? It's the first time that anyone from this school has been in a talent contest! And I am singing in English so it is good practice for us all!'

Your headmaster says, 'Well, it is a school day! I will have to speak to your class teacher and ask his opinion!'

Later that day, your class teacher says, 'You can all go to the talent contest but you must all do extra work in Mathematics at home instead, so that you don't miss any school work!'

You and your friends are really happy. You are really looking forward to it and you all spend ages discussing what you are going to wear and what you are going to sing.

At last, the day of the talent contest comes! Turn to **42**.

27

Well, you decided not to phone your father. Suddenly, the door opens. It is your father! How did he find you? Well, it is not difficult – you are in the best restaurant in town and you suppose that he must have guessed quite easily. You suddenly feel very young and stupid. Turn to **20**.

28

The door opens. You cannot believe your eyes – Paul Brown, the lead singer of the Tektroniks, walks in.

He says, 'Hi, Fonzi! How are you? Shame you couldn't come to the party but never mind, I'm sure you'll go to lots of parties when you're famous.' He winks at you.

You go the colour of a tomato – you blush and

then you ask him, 'Are you going to make a record here, too?'

He says, 'Yes, I am! I don't have the chance to play the guitar much on records so I'm going to do the backing for you!'

You are so surprised that you sit there with your mouth open!

'You?' You manage to squeak like a mouse.

He laughs, 'Yes, me. Is that OK?'

You cannot believe it. You are actually going to make a record with one of the Tektroniks! And with your favourite member of the group as well! Turn to **67**.

29

You decided not to post the letter. You have decided to go to the recording studios and that is that. You are going to take the day off school, without permission of course. You are going to miss your English and Maths exams.

The second of July arrives. It is a beautiful sunny day. You get ready to go to school as usual but of course you are not going there – you are going to the recording studios by train. You hide your blue jeans and a sweatshirt in your school bag and leave the house at the normal time. You feel a bit nervous and a bit worried about lying to your parents. Turn to **80**.

30

It is 6 May, the day of the talent contest. You get dressed and try to make yourself look like a rock star. You feel terribly nervous and on the way to the contest, sitting in a train by yourself, you wish your friends were with you.

You say to yourself, 'I should have asked the head-master! I wish I had!'

You arrive at the talent contest– you are number thirty-seven. The Tektroniks are already on stage. You receive your instructions from an organizer – you take your seat.

It begins – you are watching.

You think everyone is much older and better than you – nobody looks as nervous as you do! Your stomach feels very strange – you go to the cloakroom. You decide you cannot go on stage – you are just not good enough. Your friends are not there, so you decide to go home. Perhaps you should have taken a different route. Turn back to **17**.

31

You come back to the studio and you go into a room full of machines. The technicians, the record producer and Paul Brown of the Tektroniks are in the

room. You sit down and the producer says, 'Right, everybody, listen to this.'

He switches on a very large tape recorder and suddenly you hear your voice accompanied by a fantastic guitar. It sounds great – surely that cannot be your voice? Everybody is smiling and tapping their feet in time to the music. The producer says, 'Well, what do you think?' He looks directly at Paul Brown, and you wait anxiously. You hope that he is going to say something nice. Turn to **79**.

32

It is 20 July, the day you are going to the studios. You are really excited! You cannot decide what to wear. You try on loads of different things and finally you decide to wear your jeans and a sweatshirt. (At least you will feel comfortable.)

You are ready to go by 9 a.m. The car is not coming until 10 a.m. You keep jumping up to look out of the window. You are driving your parents mad. Your mother tells you to sit down ten times at least.

At last, a car stops outside your door and you dash outside with your father following you. It is the car from the studios. You say goodbye to your parents. Off you go. Turn to **83**.

33

You decided not to go to the talent contest. You feel
very down and very angry with your mother. You are
rude to all your friends at school. They ask you,
'What's the matter with you?'

You explain, 'My mother doesn't want me to go to
the talent contest. She doesn't think that I'm good
enough.'

Your friends say, 'Go on, Fonzi! Go – it's a really
good chance. You might be famous!'

Peter says, 'Yes, go on, Fonzi! You must go. No one
in this village has ever won anything. No one has ever
done anything exciting. Go on, you must!'

You still do not know what to do. If you decide to
go, turn to **42**. If you decide not to go, turn to **72**.

34

You turn the colour of a tomato! You blush and say,
'Yes, it's me.'

Your teacher asks you, 'Have you ever sung with
a band?'

You say, 'Well, yes. Singing is actually my hobby.'

The lesson is just ending by now and all the others
are leaving the classroom. You decide to stay on and
chat to the teacher and tell her all about the talent

contest and your problems with your class teacher. Turn to **65**.

35

You come back from lunch and you go to a big room full of people and full of lots of complicated machines. You see Paul Brown of the Tektroniks, and you blush. He says, 'Hi, Fonzi! We've just been listening to your record and it's great! Come and sit down and listen to it.'

You sit as near to Paul Brown as you can. Simon, the producer, switches on the tape. You hear your voice accompanied by some really good guitar. It sounds really different – you have never heard yourself on tape before. At the end of the song everybody claps – you feel as if you are never going to stop blushing.

Paul Brown says, 'Hey, Fonzi! I've had a great idea. We're doing a concert here on Saturday. Why don't you come up on stage with us and sing that song?' You do not know what to say, it is all too much for you! You manage to nod your head!

Simon says, 'Yeah, good idea! Then we can release the record she's just made. It's really good publicity for Fonzi.'

You feel so excited. You are actually going to sing at a concert with the Tektroniks and release a record! Turn to **75**.

36

The singer of the Tektroniks, Paul Brown, says into the microphone, 'And now, we'd like to give the prize for the best performer in the whole concert. We think the person who gave the best performance overall today is – Fonzi.' It is you! You blush and burst into tears of happiness. He takes your arm and holds it up! The audience cheers and claps. You bow and wave. Photographers are there with their flashes – clicking away.

Paul Brown says, 'Come on. There's a party backstage for the winners. We also have to talk to the record company. Winning the first prize means you are going to make a record!'

You say, 'I have to tell my friends. I'm here with my school.'

He says, 'Bring them too!'

You go back to your seat, lots of people congratulate you on the way. Your friends all kiss and hug you. You tell them about the party. Your headmaster says, 'Well done, Fonzi! But we must go back now because tomorrow is a school day, so I'm afraid you can't go to the party!'

If you decide to ignore your headmaster and go to the party, turn to **76**. If you decide to listen to your headmaster, turn to **55**.

37

You decided to listen to your parents. You all go and see your headmaster. He agrees to let you have a reasonable amount of time off from school, and you agree to work harder and concentrate on the subjects at school which are difficult for you.

Meanwhile your record climbs up and up in the charts, and you are selling more and more records. Obviously this is partly because you are lucky enough to have Paul Brown of the Tektroniks playing with you!

Well, you made the right decision. You are going to finish your education and you are continuing with your music. The biggest record magazine has a picture of you with Paul Brown on the front cover. The headlines are: 'ROCK STAR – NEW DISCOVERY!' You have made it – good luck in the future!

38

You look at the entry form. It looks quite difficult to fill in. It asks you a lot of questions about your singing.

'How long have you been singing?'

'Have you ever had singing lessons?'

'Have you ever sung in public?'

'How many people are there in your group?'

You do not really know what to say on the form. You feel very silly. You ask all your friends, 'What shall I do?'

Everybody says, 'You're crazy! You're only a kid. You're not going to win. Just forget it!'

Except your best friend Peter – he says, 'Go on! Fill it in! You are a really good singer!'

For the next few days, you keep looking at the form. You cannot make up your mind, you do not know what to do.

At last, you think, 'Why not!' You fill in the form, take it to the post office and post it. Turn to **23**.

39

You get home from school. You tell your mother what happened at school. She says, 'Well, I think you should let your headmaster decide. You need to work hard at school. Your music is just a hobby. It will never be a career. You *must* study harder.'

You feel your mother will never understand how important singing is to you. You do not say anything else to her but you just go up to your room. You sit there, look at the pictures of the Tektroniks on the wall and dream that it is you up there in the pictures.

The next day, you get up early; you are actually looking forward to going back to school – this makes a great change. You wonder what will happen. Peter and you chat and daydream about the future. 'Just imagine, you might be famous!'

You say, 'Then you can be my manager and we'll visit lots of interesting places!'

At school, you look for your English teacher. She comes into the classroom and says, 'Come with me. The headmaster wants to see you.'

You feel very nervous, all your friends are looking at you. You go to the headmaster's room, and – to your surprise – he tells you that he loves music and not only can you go to the talent contest, but he and the school are also coming to watch you. You feel very proud and also very embarrassed. Turn to **42**.

40

So, you decided to be brave and walk into the restaurant. It is quite difficult, and you feel rather strange. You have never walked into a restaurant like this before, all by yourself. You try to make yourself look older and more sophisticated – you walk in – the waiter walks over to you. He says, 'Hello! Can I help you? Are you meeting someone here?'

You say, 'Yes. I have been invited by some friends – there they are, over there.'

The waiter says, 'Are you sure?'

You feel very embarrassed. You feel as though you should not be there but you decide to walk over to where the Tektroniks and their friends are sitting – you were invited after all.

You cannot now go back and wait at the station, it is too late. Your father, wouldn't still be there. You are stuck in this situation. Especially now that the Tektroniks and several other people in their group have noticed you!

They say, 'Well, it's Fonzi! We're really pleased you came. Come and sit down. What would you like to eat?'

You say, 'Er ... er ... I don't know!'

You think you are behaving really stupidly but you do not know what to say, so you ask the person next to you, 'What are you eating? That looks very nice.'

She tells you what she is eating. You have never heard of it but you say that you will have the same. You feel really uncomfortable in this situation, if you decide to phone your father, turn to **60**. If you decide not to phone your father, turn to **27**.

41

You feel quite shocked and you do not know what to say. You try to make excuses. You say, 'But, you know, I'm not a child any more. Why should I go and see the headmaster? I haven't done anything different from my friends, Richard and James.'

Your father says, 'Richard and James! So they are your new friends! Now I understand. So you're not doing any work. You think it's clever to do nothing. Well, think again, Fonzi! I'm not letting you ruin your future. You can forget about music and lazing around until you've finished school. You and I are going to go and see the headmaster together and tell him that.'

You feel angry but also quite relieved. Life *has* been a bit difficult lately. None of your old friends has talked to you for ages – you are not invited round to their houses any longer – maybe it would be better for you to wait another couple of years, until you have finished school, before you think about music as a career. Your voice will not disappear – you can always continue to practise your singing and make a record later.

Well, this is the end of the road for you! You made a sensible decision and life returns to normal! You feel much happier! ■

42

It is 6 May, the day of the talent contest. You have arrived at the theatre – there are big posters everywhere of the Tektroniks because they are the judges of the contest. The slogans on the posters say:

HAVE YOU GOT A GOOD VOICE?

DO YOU WANT TO BE A STAR?

COME AND BE DISCOVERED!

You feel very nervous. You, your friends, your English teacher and headmaster sit down and start to watch the contest. You are number thirty-seven, so you know you have some time to wait. You bite your nails, your stomach feels very strange, you think you might be sick! You get up very quickly and go to the cloakroom. There are other contestants in there, they all seem to know each other. You feel very left out and shy. You cannot possibly go on stage! If you decide to stay in the cloakroom, turn to **18**. If you decide to be brave and carry on, turn to **21**.

43

You decided you could not go into the restaurant by yourself – you feel too shy and too young.

You hurry back to the station. You hope very much that your father has not arrived there before you. The

walk back to the station is awful – you think everybody is looking at you, so you run most of the way.

At last, you see the station and you run to the
waiting room. You cannot see your father – perhaps
he has not got there yet. Turn to **91**.

44

You decided to wait for the train for two hours. You
are already very late and you left your friends hours
ago. You feel very alone and you now have enough
time to think about what you have done. Turn to **8**.

45

You ran to your room and slammed the door. That
was not very polite of you. Your parents are only
trying to help you.

Your mother walks into the room and says, 'You
can stay at home! You're not going to the studio
because you are behaving like a spoilt baby.'

You realize you have gone too far, so you apologize
and go back into the sitting-room with your mother.
You wait to see what happens. Turn to **61**.

46

You decided to wait and discuss the problem with your father. Meanwhile, you sit down and try to concentrate on doing your homework. You find it quite impossible because you keep day-dreaming about the studios.

Finally, your father comes home and you tell him all about the letter from the studios. He is very happy for you and congratulates you, but then your mother tells him that you have exams on the same day.

He says, 'Oh dear. Well, I'm afraid you can't go to the studios then. Your education comes first.'

What do you say? If you say, 'I'm sick of school! I want to leave. My music is much more important', turn to **89**. If you say, 'Can't we talk to the headmaster and work something out?' turn to **14**.

47

The concert has finished. Now it is time to hear the results. The judges – the Tektroniks – left the stage half an hour ago. Everyone is getting really nervous and tense.

Suddenly, there is a murmur of excitement – the Tektroniks have come back on stage.

Although you think you do not have much chance, you still hope you have won something. Your friends have been telling you, 'You must win something. You were really good, miles better than the other singers!'

The Tektroniks start to read out the results. There are several sections in the talent contest for guitarists, for drummers and for singers. For each section there is a prize and there is going to be one outright winner for the whole talent contest.

You listen to the results – you do not pay much attention. You are waiting for the singing section – they are reading it out. You wait – your friends are sitting on the edge of their seats.

Third place – it is not you.

Second place – it is not you.

First place – it is YOU!

Your friends are cheering – they push you out of your seat and towards the stage – you have won! You are half laughing and half crying. You stumble on to the stage, the lead singer of the Tektroniks con-

58

gratulates you and gives you a silver cup. He says, 'Don't go away, just stay here a minute!' Turn to **36**.

48

Well, you decided not to tell your teacher about the talent contest. You spend the rest of the day at school, doing the usual boring lessons. All day your friends, especially Peter, keep saying to you, 'Come on Fonzi, why don't you go? Why don't you talk to Mrs Harrison?' (your English teacher) 'Maybe she can help you!'

At last, it is the end of the school day and you go home. Your mother says to you, 'What's the matter, Fonzi? You look so miserable!'

You say, 'Nothing, I'm all right!' You go to your room and try to do your homework. You cannot concentrate – you keep looking at your posters of the Tektroniks. You really want to see them – you really want to go to the talent contest too.

Somebody knocks at your door and then walks in. It is your father. He has just come home from work and has obviously just been talking to your mother. He asks you, 'What's all this about a talent contest?'

You tell him all about it and how much you want to go and he says, 'Well, I think you're good but I don't know *how* good you are! If you like, I'll go to school and talk to your teacher and see if we can't sort something out! Perhaps you will be able to go. You know, I used to love singing when I was your age!'

You are very grateful and thank him. Turn to **17**.

49

You go to school the next day. Everybody has heard your record on the radio. Your friends congratulate you – they are really pleased for you. Some kids are jealous, of course. They make horrible comments and make fun of you and your singing. But you are so happy that you do not care. As the days go by your record climbs into the charts – it is now in the Top Twenty!

Phonograph writes to you and tells you to contact them because you have been invited to appear on a TV rock music programme. Turn to **68**.

50

You decided to explain what you feel to your parents.
You say, 'I'm really fed up with going to school. I love
music so much and I would like to go on singing. It's
the most important thing in the world for me. School
is so boring.'

Your mother says, 'Look, Fonzi, I didn't know you
were so good at singing and I think it's wonderful.
I really understand how you feel about school but I
think you should continue going to school. Surely
you can sing and go to school as well?'

Your father says, 'I agree with your mother. You
can do both. I'll even be your manager while you are
still so young. But you must promise me that you'll
finish your education. Then, at least, if your music
isn't successful, you'll always have something else to
fall back on. Let's go and talk to your headmaster and
try and solve this problem.'

What do you do? Do you listen to your parents?
Of course you do. Turn to **37**.

51

Unfortunately your class teacher, who is a very
boring person, has heard everything and, as usual,

has not understood anything he has heard. He says, 'You can't go to the talent contest. You don't work hard enough so you can't have any time off!'

You say, 'But it's really important! Please let me take the afternoon off. I have to go to the next town for the contest and it takes a long time to get there!'

Your teacher says, 'The sixth of May – the day of the talent contest – is a school day. You must stay at school in the afternoon and do extra work in Mathematics to catch up with the others.'

You think you are going to cry. You feel very angry and very upset. You go quickly to the cloakroom and lock the door. After about five minutes, someone bangs on the door and calls your name, 'Fonzi, Fonzi!'

You think it might be your teacher. If you decide to answer, turn to **3**. If you decide not to answer, turn to **7**.

| **52** |

You say nothing and wait for your father to finish his conversation. He does not speak to you and you feel more and more tired. You think you might fall asleep.

Finally, he gets up and says goodbye to everybody.

You do the same and then you leave the restaurant together. You get into the car with your father. He is very quiet and you can tell that he is very angry. You feel frightened when you remember what you have done! Turn to **9**.

53

You all start singing. You are really enjoying yourself. Your friends stare at you because you are actually singing much louder and better than anyone else. Your teacher says, 'Who is that? Is that you, Fonzi? Who has got that incredible voice?' Turn to **34**.

54

Your father asks the producer, 'What about a contract?'

They have a conversation about financial matters. This does not really interest you, although you would be happy with just a bit more money so that you can buy clothes and records. While your father is talking, you sit and chat to Paul Brown and the others. You have to keep pinching yourself to prove that this is not a dream! Yes, it is really happening.

All too soon for you, it is time to say goodbye and you and your father go home and tell your mother all about it. Turn to **85**.

55

Well, you decided to listen to your headmaster but you would still like to try and make him change his mind!

You think it is worth talking to him. You would not feel comfortable just ignoring him so you decide to go and discuss it with him and tell him how you feel. Turn to **12**.

56

You decided to talk to Peter. He says, 'Fonzi, please listen! All your friends think you are getting too big-headed! We all like you and want you to become a star! But we can't talk to you any more. You're somewhere else, not here with us – you're in a big dream! You're no fun any more. We don't think you're our friend any longer!'

You say, 'I'm sorry, you're right. Of course I am your friend. I just keep thinking about what has happened and wondering why the record company hasn't written to me. That's why you think I'm not being friendly!'

Peter and your friends are happy you feel like this. You all get on much better and everything is like it was before! You feel happy too and life is great!

One day, when you get home from school, your mother tells you that there is a letter for you from Phonograph. Phonograph is the Tektroniks' recording company! Turn to **2**.

57

Unfortunately for you, when you arrive at the station, your father is already there and very angry indeed.

He says, 'That is really enough! How can you behave like this? Enough music, enough singing! You are going home now and you are going to study! No more going out and no more talent contests! It's finished.'

Well, this is the end of the road for you – you cannot disobey your parents however much you want to! Maybe you can try singing as a career in the future – but definitely not now!! ■

58

You decided not to join in the singing, even though you love the Beatles' songs, and especially 'When I'm sixty-four'. You listen to everyone else singing but you think you can sing much better! All your friends are looking at you. They are wondering why you have

not joined in! Finally Peter, your friend, says, 'Why didn't you sing too? You know you love that song! What's the matter with you? You are being really stupid! You are not Maria Callas yet, you know!'

Your English teacher smiles at the class and says, 'There are only five minutes until the end of the lesson? Shall we sing it again?'

Everybody says, 'Yes!' As long as nobody has to do boring grammar, they are happy! You decide to join in. Your teacher looks around in surprise when you sing. Your friend Peter is smiling at you. Your teacher says, 'Who is that singing? Is that you, Fonzi?' Turn to **34**.

59

You are asked to come and talk to the headmaster. He was at the talent contest, and he knows about your frequent absences from school. He knows, too, that you have to choose if you are going to stay at school or not!

You are not doing enough work at school and your parents are very worried. What are you going to do? You decide to talk to your parents before you go and see the headmaster. Turn to **73**.

60

You decided to phone your father. That is a really good idea. You feel very uncomfortable at the restaurant and you would prefer to be at home. You find a phone in the restaurant and you ask the waiter for the exact address. You phone home and tell your mother exactly where you are.

You say, 'Mum! Please phone the station because Dad is going to meet me there. Tell him where I am, so that he can come and pick me up here instead.' You then give her the address of the restaurant.

She writes down the details and then she says to you, 'All right, I've got the address. Now tell me how you are. Are you sure you're OK?'

You feel a bit impatient. Your mother always says this whenever you phone her from somewhere else. She worries about you too much. You say, 'Yes, of course I am. I'm not a baby, you know!'

After you have finished your phone call, you go back to your seat and wait. You sit at the same table as the Tektroniks and their friends – you have dreamed of this moment so many times and you have even thought of what you would say to the Tektroniks. But you feel very out of place and very strange and for once you wish you were at home! It seems to take ages for your father to come.

The Tektroniks offer you something to eat, but you do not know what to have. You say, 'I'll have the

same as her!' – the same as the girl you are sitting next to. Your food comes and you try to eat it, but you do not really like it. You are so tired. You really wish your father would come so that you can go home.

Finally, you see your father walking into the restaurant. He talks to the waiter for a while and then comes over to the table you are sitting at. He says, 'Hello' and starts talking to the Tektroniks and their friends. You feel very fed up and you are very tired. You are longing to go home – what do you do?

If you say, 'Come on, Dad, let's go!' turn to **22**. If you say nothing and decide to wait for your father until he is ready to go, turn to **52**.

61

Your father goes out of the house and tries the car again. This time it starts and you run out of the house, jump into the car and off you go. The garage obviously told him what to do, and it worked. Thank goodness!

You got so nervous about the problem with the car that by the time you arrive at the studio you do not feel worried any more. You get out of the car and walk into the studio with your father.

It is a very large modern place and the reception area looks more like a hotel foyer than a studio. A

middle-aged man wearing jeans comes to meet you. Your father introduces himself and you. Then he says, 'I wondered if I could stay too! I've never been to a studio before and I'd like to see how you make a record.'

The man whose name is Joe says, 'Yes, of course. Please stay. You're welcome.'

He takes you both to a room and explains what is going to happen. He wants you to sing the song you sang at the talent contest. He tells you the guitarist who is going to accompany you is just coming. You wonder who the guitarist will be! Turn to **28**.

62

You decided to leave school. You have made a big mistake. You can sing very well but you do not know what will happen. You have no education, no qualifications, nothing to fall back on. You made a wrong decision, go back to **73** and think again.

63

You decided to go back to the theatre and then go on to the restaurant with everyone else. But first you telephone your father and tell him what has happened – that there is no train for two hours and that you will wait for him at the station. You cannot tell him that you are really going back to the theatre because you know that he will be very angry. You get back to the theatre but unfortunately everyone has already left. However, you think you know the restaurant where everyone has gone, so you decide to go there.

You walk there as it is not far, but on the way you suddenly feel rather shy and unsure of yourself. You have never walked into a restaurant in a town by yourself before and you feel more and more nervous as each minute passes.

You arrive at the restaurant, it looks very large and sophisticated. You look in through the window – the Tektroniks are there with several other people. They are all enjoying themselves and laughing and joking a lot. What are you going to do? If you decide to be brave and walk in, turn to **40**. If you decide you are too shy and you cannot possibly walk in, turn to **43**.

64

Well, you sang brilliantly at the concert and all your friends and your parents think you were great! Simon Jackson, the record producer, told you at the concert that your record would be in the shops by next week. Best of all, a record magazine has interviewed you.

You are on the front cover and the headlines are:
'ROCK STAR — NEW DISCOVERY!'

You have made it – you are going to be famous!
Good luck in the future!

65

You decided to tell your English teacher all about the
talent contest. You say, 'Can I have a word with you,
please?'

The teacher says, 'Yes, of course. Come and see me
at the end of school.'

You thank her and then spend the rest of the day
wondering how you are going to tell her. It is the end
of the school day and you go to the teacher's room.
She is waiting for you. You explain everything. She
is very kind and obviously understands everything
and how you feel. She says she will speak to the
headmaster about it. She is really trying to help you.
She says, 'You've got a very good voice. You sing in

English so it's very good practice for you. I'll try and help you if I can!'

You feel very happy and answer, 'When shall I come and see you again? You know the talent contest is later this month?'

She says, 'Come and see me tomorrow at the same time and I'll tell you what happened.'

You feel very excited and hope that everything will be all right. Turn to **39**.

66

Your headmaster phones your parents. They come to the school. Everybody says they are very cross with you. Your parents and your headmaster finish by saying 'OK, Fonzi, we've had enough! We've been very supportive but now you've gone too far. You can forget about your career in music until you've finished your education.'

Well, this is the end of the road for you. You have to do what your parents and headmaster tell you. You have to finish your education first and then you can think about your singing. Perhaps you should not have gone to the station without telling anyone. That was obviously the wrong thing to do. ■

67

So you are going to make a demo disc – a trial record – with Paul Brown of the Tektronics. How amazing! You hope you are not going to make an idiot of yourself. You hope that your voice will sound all right. Your father smiles at you and you go off to the recording studio.

The producer tells you exactly what to do and you start singing into the microphone. It is very strange for you because you have to sing the same song again and again. You have to wear headphones so you cannot hear the guitar at first, you can only hear your own voice.

After what seems like a very long time indeed, the producer says that he is satisfied with the recording and you go and have lunch. Paul Brown does not join you for lunch, much to your disappointment. You wonder where he is! Turn to **31**.

68

You show the letter to your parents and your father contacts the record company and arranges your TV spot. Fortunately, it is at the weekend and therefore does not interfere with school. But as your record climbs higher and higher in the charts you find you need to take more time off from school.

This is difficult. Your headmaster lets you have some time off but you need more and more. You find you spend less time studying, and in fact you do not enjoy studying at all now. You are having a really good time singing your hit song, meeting lots of interesting people and wearing great new clothes. It is obvious that you must choose now. Are you going to stay at school? Are you going to leave school and go into the music business? Turn to **59**.

69

You are in the concert hall. All the lights have been turned off. The spotlights are on the stage. The Tektroniks walk on, and you wait at the side of the stage.

Everybody claps loudly. Then there is silence as Paul Brown, the lead singer speaks. He says, 'To start our concert, we'd like to introduce you to a new singer. She's just made a record and she's here to sing us her song. Please welcome – Fonzi!'

Everybody claps and Paul Brown waves to you. You walk on to the stage. Suddenly you do not feel nervous any longer. The spotlight is on you as you start to sing. You have never sung so well! The Tektroniks accompany you – it is great!

At the end of your song the audience claps very loudly and you leave the stage and go to your seat to watch the rest of the concert. You feel as if you are walking on air! Turn to **64**.

70

Now you find out why you are wearing headphones. Simon tells you over the headphones to sing the song again and again, correcting notes here and there. You sing it at least twenty times. You are really fed up

with it when, at last, he says, 'OK! That's it! Fonzi! Off you go and have lunch while we put the backing track on.'

You leave the room and gratefully go off for lunch with the assistant producer. You are pretty tired and you feel as if you are starving. Turn to **35**.

71

You cannot run away because your headmaster has seen you. He says in a loud voice, 'Fonzi! What on earth are you doing here? You should be at school taking your exams today. Come with me at once.'

You are really in trouble now. You have no choice, so you walk back to school with your headmaster. He is obviously very angry and you are very frightened.

He says, 'Right! Go straight to my study. I'm going to phone your parents.' Turn to **66**.

72

OK. You decided not to go.

This is the end of the adventure for you. It is a bit quick, isn't it? Perhaps you could choose differently. Go back to **15** and try again.

73

You decided to talk to your parents before going to see the headmaster. Your mother says, 'You need a good education and you can't leave school now. Music is a very dangerous business. If you don't get a good education what will you do?'

Your father says, 'I think that good exam results are very important. You'll need them for the future. You mustn't give up your studies.'

Your parents have explained how they feel and you just do not know what to do. You do not really want to stay at school at all, so what are you going to do?

If you explain how you feel, turn to **50**. If you just leave school, turn to **62**.

| 74 |

You decided you could not answer your father and ran up to your room in tears. Your father and your mother follow you. Your father says, 'Now look, Fonzi! You see what I mean? You can't even answer me sensibly. How can you possibly make a decision about your music? You are far too young. I think you should wait a couple of years until you are older.'

Your mother says, 'I agree with your father. You've got into the wrong crowd at school and you're not doing any work. How are you going to manage your school work and your music? You must wait a little while.'

You agree – it has been difficult lately and you have missed Peter in particular. You would like things to be as they were before you won the contest. Maybe

'fame' came a little too early for you! So, this is the end of the road for you. Perhaps you would like to go back and try and make some different decisions! █

75

Now you are at home again. The car took you back home from the studios after the most exciting day of your life.

You have told your parents all about the record, the concert and the Tektroniks at least fifty times. You have phoned all your friends and told them the news. Everyone is really pleased and nearly as excited as you. They are all coming to the concert to see you – and, of course, the Tektroniks! You can hardly wait for Saturday. Turn to **81**.

76

You decided not to listen to your headmaster. You are going to the party and that is that! You try to persuade your friends to come with you. You say to Peter and all the others, 'Come on, let's go! It's going to be great fun. We'll never get a chance like this again!'

Peter answers, 'We can't. We'll get into terrible trouble! But still, it would be great to go! What can we do? Shall we talk to our headmaster again?'

Your friends all agree that that is the best thing to do – to talk to your headmaster. You are not sure. If you decide to talk to your headmaster again, turn to **12**. If you decide to go to the party anyway, turn to **87**.

77

What a disaster! The car will not start, and you are supposed to be at the studios at 10 a.m. What is going to happen? Your father tries to start the car again and again – nothing happens.

He says, 'I'm going to go and phone the garage. Go back into the house, Fonzi.'

By this time, you are in a panic. You say to your mother, 'Oh, no! why does something like this always happen to me?'

She says, 'Calm down, Fonzi. Your father will sort it out.'

If you run to your room and slam the door, turn to **45**. If you sit down and try to stay calm, turn to **61**.

78

Well, you decided to go to the restaurant. You are really enjoying yourself and for once you feel very important. You know very well that you should not be there – you should have gone when your friends left, back to your village with your school. You feel a little bit guilty and wonder how you are going to get home.

Everybody is talking to you, including the Tektroniks. Soon they start discussing food and what they are going to eat. You suddenly realize that you have no money at all! What on earth are you going to do? You cannot afford to eat anything at all, and not only that – how are you going to get home? You feel very young and very stupid! HELP! Turn to **6**.

79

Paul Brown of the Tektroniks is going to say something about the demo disc you just made together. This could affect your whole future.

He says, 'I think the record's fantastic! Why don't we release it as a proper record? I'm sure it'll sell a million.'

Everybody agrees and says, 'Yes, what a great idea!' 'Yes, let's do that.' 'It would certainly sell with your name on it, Paul. And Fonzi's got a great voice!'

You feel really excited. You want to get up and dance around the room. But you obviously do not do that – it would look extremely silly! Turn to **54**.

80

You walk straight to the station and you hope you will not meet any of your teachers. You go by the small side streets, hoping not to see anyone you know.

You arrive at the station. You buy a ticket and go and wait on the platform. You hope no one will notice you. You decide you are going to get changed into your jeans in the washroom on the train.

You wait, but of course the train is late. You sit and bite your nails. You feel very nervous. At last, the train arrives. You go towards the train door and wait for the people to get off. Horrors! Oh, how awful! There is your headmaster, just getting off the train and he has seen you! Turn to **71**.

81

It is Saturday, the day of the concert. A car is coming to collect you and your parents. Your mother has made you a fabulous costume to wear on stage. All your friends have already left for the next town to go to the concert! The car arrives and you and your parents get in. You feel really excited and just a bit nervous. Your parents say, 'You'll be all right, Fonzi. Just keep calm. We're really proud of you.'

You find it difficult to sit still – you cannot wait to get there. Turn to **69**.

82

So you decided to be sensible and go back to your village. You leave the theatre and walk towards the station. You feel really happy and, for once in your life, really important. You get to the station – you have missed the train! There is not another train for two hours. If you decide to wait for two hours, turn to **44**. If you decide you might as well go back to the theatre and go to the restaurant with the others, turn to **63**.

83

You arrive at the studios and get out of the car. It was great, riding in the big car. You felt like a queen!

The producer comes out to meet you and introduces himself, 'Hi, I'm Simon Jackson. You must be Fonzi. I'm looking forward to working with you. I've

heard a lot about your singing from Paul Brown. He's coming in today, you know.'

You feel really excited because you are going to see the Tektroniks again. You just manage to say, 'Really?'

You go inside the studios and go to a room where there is just a microphone and a chair. Simon, the producer, tells you to put on the headphones and sing the song with which you won the talent contest. You must sing into the microphone. He then leaves the room. You feel a bit silly in the room, all by your-self, but when you start singing it is OK. Turn to **70**.

84

You did not sleep very well and you still feel very down. You get up and get ready for school slowly; you know that you have to talk to your father.

You go to have your breakfast. Your father is sitting there waiting for you. At once, you stop feeling hungry. You sit down and your mother gives you your breakfast, but you cannot eat it. You know your father will start speaking to you. He says, 'I've been talking to your mother. The date for your demo disc is the second of July. That is the same date as your English and Maths exams. I think it would be better for your future if you decided to cancel the recording studio.'

You say, 'I can't do that. It's really important. I probably won't get another chance.'

Your father says, 'I'll write a letter to the recording studio now and you can post it on the way to school. The studio can easily give you another date.' He writes the letter and gives it to you to post. If you decide to post it, turn to **5**. If you decide not to post it, turn to **29**.

85

So, after all the excitement it is back to school and a normal life for you. Of course you tell your friends all about it, but for a long time life continues as usual and you hear nothing from Phonograph. At least you passed all your exams at school so you have no problems there.

One day when you turn on the radio at home you hear the disc jockey say, 'And here's a great new record by Paul Brown of – need I say it – the Tektroniks! And singing with him is a wonderful new discovery – Fonzi! I think we'll be hearing a lot more from this talented young lady.'

He plays the record. You cannot believe it and you call your parents, 'Come here, quickly! Listen! It's me on the radio! Quick!'

You all listen to the radio. You are so happy you could burst! Your parents are delighted too. Turn to **49**.

86

You decided to wait for your father. You sit in the waiting-room and look around for something to read. There are a few people in the waiting-room as well as you but there is nobody who is as young as you. You wait for ages – you feel really uncomfortable and you wish your father would hurry up and come.

After sitting in the waiting-room for a long time, a familiar figure walks in. It is your father. You are so pleased to see him that you jump up and run towards him.

He says to you, 'You silly girl! Come on, let's go home now!'

He is not angry with you at all and soon you are safely at home and in your room. Turn to **25**.

87

Well, here you are at the party. Your friends did not want to come with you. They decided they did not dare come with you. They have gone back to the

village with your headmaster and the school. You hope nobody will notice your absence.

Peter, your best friend, said before he left, 'Gosh! You're brave! I wouldn't like to be in your shoes when our headmaster finds out that you're not with us!'

You feel rather shy at the party. You stay near the door and you hope that someone will notice you. Someone does – Paul Brown – the singer of the Tektroniks. He says, 'Hey, look everybody, here's Fonzi. Isn't she great!'

You feel very embarrassed at this but lots of people come towards you. They introduce themselves. You are so excited and happy that you forget their names immediately. They ask you questions like, 'How long have you been singing?', 'Have you got a band?', 'Are you going to make a record?'

You are really surprised and very pleased that all these sophisticated people are so interested in you. They are all so much older and more fashionable than you. You talk to them for ages and then someone says, 'How about going to a restaurant for

something to eat? I don't know about you but I'm starving!'

You do not know what to do. You would love to go but you should really catch the train and go back to your village. If you decide to go to the restaurant, turn to **78**. If you decide to go back to your village, turn to **82**.

88

Your headmaster was very understanding! You study very hard for your exams and take them one day early.

At last it is the day you are going to the recording studios. It is a beautiful day and you wake up very early. You feel rather nervous, but fortunately your father is going with you.

You try to eat some breakfast but you have butterflies in your stomach because you are so nervous and you can only manage to eat a little.

You go to your room and try to decide what you are going to wear. You change your mind hundreds of times and soon your bed is covered in clothes. Finally you decide to wear your blue jeans and a

sweatshirt. You may not look glamorous and sophisticated but at least you are comfortable! It is time to leave, so you say goodbye to your mother and you wave to your friends, who are just walking past your house on their way to school. They shout, 'Good luck! Good luck, Fonzi! We'll keep our fingers crossed!'

You jump into the car next to your father. You are ready to go! Splut – bang – the car will not start! Turn to **77**.

89

You told your parents that you were fed up with school.

Your father is very angry with you and says, 'Now, look here, Fonzi. You are too young to make any decisions. For a long time now, you've just been concentrating on your music. I think it's time to concentrate on your studies too. You can lose your voice but you won't lose your education. Forget about your music for now. You can always come back to it later. So – no studios – no demo disc!'

You are very angry and really upset. Unfortunately, this is the end of the road for you – maybe it is better for you to concentrate on your studies now. But it does make you unhappy. Perhaps you would like to go back to **46** and make a different decision.

90

So you decided not to wait for your father – you want to go the restaurant. You know where it is, even if you do not know the address. You want to see what is happening, and you also want to take part in it!

You walk to the restaurant by yourself and you feel rather strange and very young and very unsure of yourself. You think everybody is looking at you and wondering what you are doing by yourself in the town.

You get to the restaurant at last. It looks very elegant and big. You look in at the windows. The Tektroniks are there with a group of other people. They are all laughing and talking. You decide you cannot possibly go in and you decide to go back to the station and wait for your father. Turn to **57**.

91

You are in the waiting-room. Perhaps your father has not arrived yet. Suddenly, the door swings open. Your father walks in. He looks extremely angry.

He says, 'Fonzi, that is really enough! How can you behave like this? Enough music, enough singing! You're going home now and you're going to study.

No more going out and definitely no more talent contests. It's all over for you!'

Well, this is the end of the road for you. You cannot disobey your parents, however much you want to. Maybe you can try singing as a career in the future, but certainly not now! ■

GLOSSARY

ages; for ages for a long time

amazing; how amazing you think it's wonderful

backing musical accompaniment

band rock group

big-headed you think you are better than anyone else

bothered; you cannot be bothered it's too much trouble for you

burst; you could burst you feel very excited

contest competition

demo disc a test record

to fall back on to rely or depend on

to feel down to feel depressed

to feel left out to feel ignored

to get through to contact on the phone

to have butterflies in your stomach to feel frightened

to keep fingers crossed for good luck

to laze around to do no work

longing; you are longing to you really want to

to make up your mind to decide

moon; to be over the moon to feel very happy

to mutter to speak very quietly

over; it's all over for you it's finished, there's nothing more you can do

pinch; to keep pinching yourself to squeeze a fold

of your skin in order to make sure that you are still
awake

poster advertisement

to ring to phone

rude impolite

to be sick to feel ill

to sort it out to solve the problem

starving to feel very hungry

thumb; to give a thumbs-up sign for good luck

TV spot TV appearance

walk; to feel as if you are walking on air to feel
very happy because you have done something well

word; can I have a word with you? can I speak to
you?